the Puzzle

JANET L. ADAMS

PAGE PUBLISHING
Conneaut Lake, PA

First originally published by Page Publishing 2023

ISBN 979-8-88793-274-3 (pbk)
ISBN 979-8-88793-279-8 (digital)

Printed in the United States of America

The Puzzle is dedicated to my husband, Paul, who always encourages me, appreciates me, and loves me beyond measure. God placed him in my life to complete my puzzle, and I am forever grateful.

CONTENTS

CHAPTER 1

Discontent

Although I was happy with my husband and family, I felt like I had fallen into a constant rerun of my daily life. I was beginning to question everything in my mind. What was the purpose? Was I living or just existing? I had been married to Jacob for a little over fourteen years, and our love was stronger than ever, though bland. I wanted something to spice up our relationship. The mundane routine of life was becoming so laborious. Each day brought the same repetition of unsatisfying tasks. After all, one can only get so excited about the perfect crease on a pant leg or the mirror shine in the pane windows.

On the other hand, I felt blessed that nothing was upsetting the boat. We were healthy, financially sound, and strong. That is definitely something for which to be thankful even though I felt so needed, I felt so unappreciated. The kids were at the stage of life where they needed me but not for anything glamorous or exciting. I desired more in my life, and I didn't know what that was. I looked toward Jacob to fill that emptiness. We still bonded with each other in a way that I don't think we even understood. I wanted, *no, craved* something more. I wanted others to wonder what kept our relationship so good. Yes, that would be a challenge at this time of my life. It became my obsession, not just to prove to others our eternal love but also to reassure myself.

We met when we were nineteen during the second semester of college. Both of us had not dated a lot during our high school years. I wasn't into the casual dating scene. I wanted a connection for the future. I dated a few guys whom I thought would be a good catch, but I realized that they were high school boys with active sexual desires, and I just wasn't going to make them come true. I wanted to date my future commitment, my forever man.

Jacob, on the other hand, worked too hard to spend money on a date for someone that would not be a future investment. At first, I thought he came from a family that struggled financially, but that was not the case at all. His parents instilled the value of hard work and focus. He has loving, nurturing mother and father with a fervent belief in God and a strong work ethic. Both were alive and healthy and financially secure. His dad was the self-taught type who mastered just about any skill that he attempted. He set goals for himself, and his aim was set directly at reaching them. Jacob was a balance of both.

When we first met, we were instantly attracted to each other, and once we began dating, we were inseparable. We thought we were so together, but when I shuffle back through old photos, I laugh at how we looked. Jacob resembled "Grizzly Adams"—rugged and strong yet nurturing. His hair was shoulder length and wavy, and he looked sort of like a rebel. A huge smile covered his face, and joy filled his heart. He was secure in himself.

I always seemed to do what was expected of me. I never wanted to disappoint, upset, or hurt anyone. My hair was long with soft curls. I didn't wear much makeup, just mascara. The looks worked for us and for each other. We never seemed to be apart except for work and college. We developed such a strong bond and enjoyed each other's company so much that you would have thought we were joined at the hip. He was such a babe in the romance department, but it was cute. We both thought too rationally for our age.

After classes, I worked in a department store until 10:30 p.m. I would find love notes tucked under the windshield wiper; his corny innocence always touched my heart.

Jacob's personality was entertaining, to say the least. His quick-witted comments always kept everyone amused. My family instantly adored him as well. And to tell you the truth, my life has been amazing since we met. After dating for two years, we married. I still had a year to finish college, and he continued to work and save.

After college graduation, we knew that we needed to plant new roots, so we moved to Arizona. This was a tremendous shock to our families. But we totally depended on each other as family and friends were far away from us. It worked. Our relationship flourished, and we planned goals for our family and future. We set up a home in a one-bedroom apartment. Jacob established a construction business, and it seemed to blossom from the start. I interviewed for the librarian opening at the city library and was hired. Four years later, I was promoted to director. We both loved our jobs and succeeded in them. Within a year of moving, we bought two acres on the edge of town and began building our dream home. His talents and his crew made the process easy.

We found ourselves involved in physical labor as much as possible. We cleared trees and bushes. We worked as a team into the late evenings cleaning the construction site. Jacob understood every phase of construction, and if we could, we did the work ourselves. It was a fun way to build our lives together (pun intended), but it was exhausting. Our bones and muscles were maxed out each night, but the back rubs were wonderful. By the end of each day, we collapsed, but our completed home was worth it. We seemed to agree on everything in our lives. Our ideas always complimented each other. We set goals together and worked toward reaching those goals.

After being a twosome, we became parents to a sweet little girl, Jill. This event bonded us even closer as a family. It was fun to watch Jacob with Jill. He had minimal experience with babies, but he easily adapted to his new role. Life as a dad seemed to agree with him as long as he could hand Jill back to me when she needed a diaper change or when she was fussy. I accepted that.

Anyway, I knew he wasn't being chauvinistic about this; he just felt totally uncomfortable. I knew that he made mega advances in fatherhood. Even though we waited until we were financially secure, I knew that Jacob still had reservations about starting a family, but Jill stole his heart. No parents would ever ask for a sweeter, lovelier daughter. She was our greatest asset.

A little over a year later, we decided to try it again. This time we changed the nursery colors for a boy. Michael was quite different, and Jacob was so proud to have a son. He was what Dobson labels the strong-willed child. He fit the role from the beginning of his birth. Jacob said that it was probably payback from his own childhood behavior. So here we are, parents of an eight-year-old girl and a six-year-old boy. Life was great! We enjoyed attending soccer and baseball games, dance practice, church activities, and the tedious times to finish schoolwork in the evenings. We were blessed with health, successful jobs, and all the luxuries that went with both. But of course, that was our plan when we committed to each other.

Our lives revolved around work and children. Like most parents today, we started to live with the *taxi-driver* syndrome. Sometimes it became so hectic, but I didn't want a dull life. Yet my life felt uneventful in a world full of activity. Jacob's construction business was exploding with opportunity, but he seemed to have less time for us. His energy focused on work, but it *was* for our life together. I know how he operates when he has a goal. Now he had college tuition, room and board, proms, weddings, food, and clothing for his children on his mind. So without realizing it, he was providing for us financially but denying us time with him. I felt like I was losing him in some way. He still kissed me as soon as he walked through the door and hugged me while I stood at the kitchen sink washing late-night dishes. He murmured sweet words in my ear and always told me that he was happy with his life. Our sex life was fulfilling and passionate. So why was I discontent?

Now for some reason, I wanted to do something unexpected. Jacob had always said that he knew me too well—that I didn't even have to speak for him to know what I was thinking. Often times, it was true. He would blurt out what was on my mind so often. I wanted to act unpredictable, sexy, and cunning. I guess part of my feelings centered on me being in my mid-thirties. *Yuck!* I didn't feel that age. I kept thinking about what could I do that would spice my life. All through my adult life, I always thought about doing grand things, but I never followed through with any of them. I wanted to feel desirable and attractive, clever and seductive, but yet I didn't want to step out of my comfort of safety.

CHAPTER 2

The Plan

The idea came to me one evening when Jacob came home from work. He emerged in the kitchen and proudly told me that the receptionist at one of his suppliers was making the moves on him. Apparently, the new receptionist, Becky, tried to entice him with more than words. She was revealing more than the prices of windows. Initially, Jacob thought that one of the guys was playing a joke on him. It turned out it wasn't a joke, but she really was making an advance. I could tell by the minute details that he was flattered. I wasn't upset as I know his heart. This wasn't the first time that advances were made to Jacob, and it probably wasn't going to be the last. After all, Jacob did have an adorable, magnetic personality. I was pleased that he knew the right response and not the typical *guy* response. In almost two decades of knowing him, I only met one person with whom he had a conflict.

He never hid these temptress moves. Actually, I think he enjoyed letting me know that he was still a desirable catch. We both knew that we were committed to each other in every way. We had a bond that not many couples could say they share. As I said, we didn't date much, and when we met, we shared the same values and morals. We wanted to honor God in our relationship and decided to wait for marriage to have complete intimacy. We set our parameters and lived by them. I know many couples might not understand this, but it made perfect sense to us.

I had the perfect idea to end my restlessness. I was so caught up in the role of mother, working woman, and wife that I needed a little excitement in my life. Sure, I was fantastic at cleaning the toilets, ironing the perfect shirt, washing the floors, and running the ideal taxi service for our munchkins, but I wanted "*no* more dull and mundane!" *Help*! I just desired some flavor in my life.

It came to me so clearly: What if I would be the next person to seduce him, like a secret admirer? Then on our fifteenth anniversary, I would reveal myself to him. I began to plot it out.

I became excited about what was conjuring up in my mind. That Saturday afternoon following Jacob's somebody-wants-me-baby story, I made plans to go shopping. I called Annie, my closest friend, and asked if the kids could spend time with her and their children. Our children have grown up together. She has a girl about a year older than Jill and twin boys a few months older than Michael. We think of them as family. We spend time together often. Usually, I would have stayed and visited with Annie, sipping on ice tea, talking, and watching the kids develop their friendships. I contemplated sharing my scheme with Annie, but I decided to keep it a secret. I was great at starting personal things, but they usually fizzled out before completion. If someone else knew, the plan might fade, and I didn't want that to happen. So Annie kept the kids, and I set out on a shopping adventure to initiate my plan.

I was a kid on a scavenger hunt trying to find the perfect dress for our anniversary dinner. I know that seven months ahead of schedule sounds a little premature, but all the pieces had to fit. When I walked through the doors of the third boutique, it was hanging against the wall. It seemed to be calling to me. "This is *it!*" It was a sleeveless black dress that plunged with a V neckline and a slightly lower V in the back. I fingered through the rack to locate the correct size. "It is a good style for any occasion. Would you like to try it on? I'm Helen. Would you like me to start a dressing room?" she spoke.

I told her, "Yes." And that I would like to browse around a little longer. But nothing caught my eye like that dress. It was so unlike me to wear a dress that was the least bit suggestive, but this was it. I entered the dressing room and tried it on. Instantly I knew that this was it. Now if I would take off those extra ten pounds that I have been holding onto, it would be perfect. I rotated from every angle.

It fell above my knees. It was the kind of dress that I wish I had the nerve to wear but would have always chosen something a little more modest. It wasn't sleazy but elegant and sexy. I couldn't believe what I was about to do.

Then Helen spoke from opposite the door, "How do you like it, honey? Is there something else I can show you?" I opened the door, and she said, "It looks fabulous on you!" I asked about shoes, and she asked for my size and swiftly left.

I continued to maneuver my body in front of the mirror to build up my confidence. Helen returned with two different pairs of black shoes. I tried the first pair, a simple black pump. But the second pair complimented the dress perfectly—a sleek line with a wide ankle strap. She asked me, "Is it for a special occasion because you look radiant?" Goose bumps covered my body at the thought of it. I told her that it was for my fifteenth anniversary. I also told her that I wanted my purchase to be a size smaller. She smiled and said, "He will love you in that, honey!" Within a few minutes, I was back in my clothes and making my purchase. Helen reassured me, "You look wonderful. Your husband will be pleased." I walked from the store like *Pretty Woman* after her shopping spree.

When I arrived home, I felt a schoolgirl expression across my face. I pulled into the garage, opened the back door, took hold of my purchases, and triumphantly walked into my house. No one was home. Jill and Michael were still over at Annie's house. I had a few minutes before she would drop them off. Jacob was checking on job sites. I strutted to my closet and hung my dress in the back so no one would see it.

Jacob never noticed when I wore something new. Why would he notice it hanging in the closet? He always complimented me on how I looked but never seemed to care what I was wearing. A few times he would say, "Why don't you wear something like that?" when he saw it in a magazine or on someone else. "You would look great in it." I didn't want to take the chance of him seeing it though. Jill was an inquisitive child, and if she saw it, she would ask questions. She was mature for her age, and sometimes it was so easy to share my thoughts with her. Michael was my true critic. Even though he was only six, he spoke truthfully about my fashion. When he liked a look, he spoke with such sincere words and expressions. I really wanted to model the dress for both of them but knew it would ruin my plan. I was still in the bedroom when I heard the kids yelling, "Mom, we're home. Where are you?"

"I'm coming!" I shouted back. I closed the closet doors and walked to the kitchen. Annie said that she had to run so I thanked her, and we said our goodbyes. That was great because she might ask me what I bought that afternoon.

Jill was full of stories from her afternoon. She tried to tell me what the boys did, but she laughed so hard that I didn't understand a word. Michael chuckled and covered his face with embarrassment. It sounded like they had a lovely afternoon.

Well, I knew if I was going to look *hot* in that dress, I better concentrate on cutting back on calories and those notorious fat grams. I knew it was going to be a challenge, but I had a purpose, a smaller size dress, and I was energized. I could see the end of the tunnel or maybe just the beginning.

I spent the next three weeks carefully measuring out portions in my mind. I didn't weigh my food because I didn't want anyone to know that I was dieting. After about a week, I felt less fluffy. I walked the treadmill and worked on the step and hated every moment of it. I could feel the difference in my clothes when I put them on. Even my coworkers mentioned how great I looked. I couldn't believe that I was actually sticking to my plan. Losing weight was something that I hated to think about, but it was part of my actual goal. I had lost about eight pounds by that point, and I felt great.

On Tuesday evening, I asked Jacob if he would watch the kids the following Saturday afternoon. I stressed how I wanted to get some Christmas shopping done. He hated shopping, especially Christmas shopping, so he agreed. When it came to gift buying for each other, we kept that simple.

Our first Christmas after our move, we had a Charlie Brown Christmas. We cut down a small pine sapling from our property that we had just purchased. It was only about four feet tall with bare spots all over. We were scrimping and saving to begin construction on our home. Jacob as well as his crew did a lot of the work. Our goal was to build the entire house without taking a loan. He worked on it when he finished his work hours.

For Valentine's Day that year, he told me that he bought me windows, and I bought him doors. It was romantic because we were actually building our life together. Every holiday or special occasion, we purchased something for the house. We even moved in before it was completed. That way we could eliminate commuting time so we would have more time to work on the small things. When I arrived home from work, I sanded the baseboards and trim. There was so much I learned about construction and the time and effort it takes to complete a task. Jacob labored in the important and more skilled jobs.

When it came to installing the floors, we had already been in the house for three months. We celebrated each building's accomplishment. Since that Christmas, we haven't bought gifts for each other for the holidays. The thought of buying because society labeled it a gift-giving day wasn't important to us. However, we both loved getting presents for the kids. Jacob bought most items for Michael while I bought for Jill. After they had gone to bed, he would pull out his purchases. He told me of his childhood toys and thoughts. Sometimes I wondered if I had three children. I guess that is one of the things I love about him—his sweet innocence.

Once he bought this high-tech toy machine gun. He had seen it about a year earlier at a client's house. It had seven different weapons in one unit. It included swords and true-life sounds. When Michael opened it, I amused myself watching how Jacob strategically maneuvered the gun from Michael. He kept saying, "Let me show you how that works," or "Did you see this feature?" He is such a levelheaded, intelligent guy, yet he can regress to a little boy. Jacob was extremely attractive to me in the role of being a dad. Men are so sexy when they show love to their kids.

He said that he had to check in on a few jobs that morning, but he agreed to be there so I could *shop*. He decided to take the kids to a movie. It was a rare treat for them, so everyone was excited to notice my mischievous expression. They were too involved in searching for a show. It was wonderful to see them supporting their reasons for their selection.

On Wednesday morning, I called and made an appointment for one thirty with a local photographer. Several of my friends were doing photo shoots so I casually asked around to find out who did a good job.

I continued to watch my eating habits. That evening I was so tempted to nibble a few bites of chocolate but knew that I might not stop. I went to the next best place—the bathroom scale. The satisfaction I saw was better than the creamy taste of chocolate. I had lost another three pounds, and it was late in the day. Jacob was still out, and Jill and Michael were involved in other activities. I slipped into my room, locked the door, and tried on my dress. It felt wonderful as it hung over my hips. I quickly returned back into the girl in rags, rehung the dress, and nonchalantly walked to the kitchen to check on dinner.

I had not been wearing anything that would cling to reveal my weight loss. I mainly operated with dim lights in front of Jacob. I know that sounds funny. Usually, I would have shared every ounce that I lost, but this was all part of my plan. I waited patiently for Saturday to arrive. I continued to eat *healthy* and drink plenty of water. I felt less puffy, and that was enough to keep me going.

CHAPTER 3

Follow Through

Saturday morning Jacob and I sat down for an early cup of coffee. We talked about business. He looked out the kitchen window at the squirrels playing chase, then he looked over at me. He affectionately said, "You look fantastic, honey!" I was unsure. Could he sense something? I walked over to him, hugged his neck from the back of his chair, and told him, "That kind of talk could get you lucky." Then I added, "later."

Then I practically shoved him out of the door. I knew that he wanted to meet Phil by eight thirty, and I didn't want him to ask any questions. I handed him an insulated mug filled with coffee and kissed him goodbye again. I reminded him to be back by twelve thirty.

The kids were mellowing their morning by watching cartoons, so I went to shower. It was kind of a lazy morning. When I came out to the kitchen, the kids were eating breakfast. Around ten, I corralled them into their rooms to make their beds and get dressed. They hadn't even combed their hair. All I had to do was remind them that they had an outing with their dad. They helped me clean up the mess. They weren't thrilled at the thought, but they responded by vacuuming, cleaning the morning dishes, and mopping the floors. We were finished a little past eleven.

I walked to the bathroom and heated the curling iron. While I waited for it to heat, I folded a load of laundry and dispensed them into the correct drawers. Oh, it was a fun life.

Just when I finished curling my hair, Jacob arrived home. You could hear his truck pull up the driveway. He came in and said that he would take the kids to lunch, so I didn't need to prepare anything. "Sounds great," I replied.

As soon as they left, I dressed in jeans and a sweatshirt. My clothes felt looser too. I went to the back of my closet where I hid the dress. I collected the dress, shoes, and under garments and headed to the door.

I drove to the photographer. My stomach was jittery, like a shy student walking on stage for a solo. I recollected my treasures and entered the building. Grace, the photographer, showed me to a dressing room. I couldn't help but smile, a timid smile while I changed into my dress.

As soon as I stepped from the dressing room, I felt like an actor getting ready for set. One person lifted my hair, twisted it, flopped it, and fluffed it. She told me that I had a lot of possibilities. For some reason, I already had a great sense of accomplishment and satisfaction even though I had no makeup. A satin robe was handed to me to put on over my dress. I was escorted to a chair and their work began. I tried to just go with all the pampering and soon found myself very relaxed. In about thirty minutes I had been transformed, like Cinderella going from rags to the princess of the ball.

They were ready for the photo shoot. There were several backdrops and vignettes. They suggested different poses with which I complied. Some felt odd, some natural. When the shoot was completed, I took down my hair and wiped some of the makeup off. They didn't overdo it, but I still couldn't return home like that. I put on my jeans and sweatshirt.

With instant photography, I was able to proof my pictures before I left. Grace told me that she would proof and photoshop where needed and put the photo stick in my mailbox by two o'clock the next day.

The staff shot me one upbeat comment after another which really boosted my confidence. I was on top of the world. I thought it would be a fun place to work—making dreams come true or getting a movie star ready for their shooting. Jacob always said that he would have enjoyed working in Hollywood creating sets. He loved animation, scenery, technology, and the reality of the *fake*. I exited like I had never been there and headed to the department store. I had to make a few purchases to back up my shopping story. We had always been honest with each other, and even though that was not my intention for my outing, I still had said that I was shopping. I actually managed to select some nice gifts.

Ironically we drove into the driveway at just about the same time. I had enough time to unlock the door and rehang my dress toward the back of the closet when I heard their chatter and laughter. Jacob, Jill, and Michael were like the Three Stooges when they walked through the kitchen. They were so excited over the day's events that Michael could barely get the words out. Before he could finish his tale, Jill chimed in with another funny tale. It took the rest of the evening to get all the details. I missed out on family fun time. I had mixed emotions about it. I could have been with my family sharing a rare moment, but I was stirred with a growing passion for enticing my own husband. I knew I would feel better once the whole sequence of events started to fall into place. Besides, I would get over it.

The next day, I was at the sink when Grace pulled up to the mailbox. I quickly ran out front, waved, and approached her car as no one was around. She handed me a small envelope with a photo stick. She told me that I wouldn't have a hard time selecting a good one as they were all amazing. I thanked her, and off she went.

I slid the envelope into my pocket and went inside the house. Everyone was occupied so I grabbed my laptop, snuggled into the corner chair, inserted the photo stick, and viewed my pictures. I was shocked at how glamourous I looked. I was vacillating between the two of them and decided that they were similar—that it didn't matter. I went to an online photo sight and placed an order for an eight-by-ten puzzle. Done! I was so excited.

I hummed a little tune as I prepared dinner that evening. The kids were in a good mood too. We all sat down to a family dinner with a lot of talk about the weekend. After dinner, I helped Jill gather up art supplies for one of her creative moments. Michael chose his favorite place on the couch as we snuggled together to read. He was really getting into reading even though he was only in kindergarten. I purposely did not teach him too much before he started school because he picks things up quickly, and he has a fall birthday. He needed challenges to keep him out of trouble. Hopefully, he would finish the year with a continued upswing.

Later that evening, I called Annie for a quick chat. I almost blurted everything to her but managed to hold it in. I wanted to share everything with her, the plan, my reasoning, my pictures, and my transformation. I felt so sneaky and so happy. When I hung up, I curled up next to Jacob.

CHAPTER 4

Setup

To make everything fall into place, I had to lay it out for perfect timing. I looked at the calendar and counted the weeks until our anniversary. I went into the office and took a spiral notebook from the cabinet. It was time to plan my secret letters as I snuggled into the corner of the couch.

For the time following the Christmas holiday, I laid out a timeline of the letters and what the content of each would be. My calculations determined that I needed ten different notes. Each quality chosen had my mind drifting to memories of Jacob. My first letter would be given on January 2, and my final letter would be on May 8, just in time for our anniversary. I wanted to randomly give them to Jacob from start to finish.

Because I am kind of artsy, I thought I would handwrite the letters, enlarging my font, but later changed my mind to use the computer. After all, Jacob knows my talents, and I didn't want him to recognize any of my scripts.

I had plenty of gift wrap and stationery but nothing that would be perfect for my plan. After all, I rarely wrote to anyone when it was easier to call or text. So I bought some powdery turquoise blue unlined stationery and a darker turquoise calligraphy marker to sign my alias. The paper was simple, resembling parchment. There were some extra sheets just in case I made a mistake.

I addressed *all* ten envelopes "Jacob" so that my writing would be the same. I didn't want to try to remember how I disguised my writing. I knew that was wise.

Christmas activities took up the next three weeks. The kids were involved in school programs, school parties, Sunday school parties, and the Christmas parade. Jacob and I attended several Christmas parties and events as well. By this point, I had lost about eighteen pounds—kind of hard to cover up the loss. It's funny how feeling good about yourself helps your mood. At each party, I felt I glowed. I don't know if it was because I held a secret, or I was just happy.

Jacob's arms wrapped around me like he didn't want to let go. He always spoke affectionately, and I reciprocated. Our connection seemed to deepen even with all the activity and functions.

All the running around, organizing, and hustling and bustling were invigorating, not drudgery or a burden. What little time was left, I wrapped presents and planned his business party, which we always held between Christmas and New Year. Luckily, most of this was arranged months ago. Sometimes I thought about giving up on my idea to seduce my husband in such an extreme way. It would have been easier, but I did not want to quit again.

When arriving home from work on Thursday, I stopped at the mailbox. A large white envelope was nestled between a catalog and letters. I pulled it out, felt the package, flipped it over, and saw that it was from the photo company. I laid it in my lap and pulled into the garage and entered the house. I tossed the rest of the mail on the table and walked to our bedroom. No one was home yet. The kids were with friends, and they were dropping them off. Jacob was still at work, naturally.

I opened the envelope and pulled out a thick plastic-wrapped puzzle. My eyes shifted from top to bottom, left to right. I loved it! It would fit into my plan perfectly. I shuffled into the office and took out eleven envelopes, one for each of my proposed letters and the final encounter.

Then I went into the bathroom and found my cuticle scissors. I slit the back of the puzzle with them and took off the wrap. I ordered a sixty-piece puzzle so that meant I would include five to six pieces with each love letter. I saved the face portion for the final encounter. I divided out all the pieces and labeled the envelopes one to eleven. I cleaned up my space and put the envelopes in my lingerie drawer.

The final preparation was complete. I was *not* going to be a quitter, so I was ready to enter the next phase of my plan on January 1.

CHAPTER 5

Why Not

Okay, twenty pounds is twenty pounds, and it took a lot of intense focus to lose it. I wanted to enjoy my new body. Besides Jacob knew I was smaller. He could feel it when he wrapped his arms around me or snuggled. My face was thinner too. So for his business Christmas party, I bought a new dress. It was a red satin slip-style dress with spaghetti straps. It stopped above my knees. I wore strappy black high heels. Again I was stepping out of my comfort zone, but I loved my new body.

Over the years, I added a bit more to my makeup routine, eyeliner, brow liner, and lipstick. I kept it subtle and natural-looking.

When I emerged from the bedroom, Jacob was standing by the couch. He looked up, and I thought I saw his jaw drop. He softly muttered, "Wow, baby!" Then he added, "You are making me want to stay home."

A smile covered my whole face, and I knew he would have swooped me up then, but we were the ones putting on the party. He walked toward me, slid his arm around my waist, pulled me in, and passionately kissed me. Well, that set the mood for the rest of the evening.

We knew that we had to get to the restaurant early to take in gifts. They were already placed in the back of our SUV.

Jacob helped me with my coat, and he turned me around for one more kiss. "You look fantastic!" he murmured in my ear. Then he opened the door, and we walked to the car. He opened my door and waited. I sat and lifted my legs into the car. "Is it okay if you are my dessert tonight?" he confidently asked. Jill and Michael were spending the night at Annie's house so we had the house to ourselves.

On the drive to the restaurant, we talked. Jacob asked, "Do you know that I am one lucky man to have you as my wife?

I teasing asked, "Why do you consider yourself lucky?"

"Because you are everything I have ever wanted. Not only are you gorgeous and sexy, but you are an amazing woman. You handle so much throughout your day, take excellent care of the kids and me, volunteer, and cook delicious meals for us every night, and you still manage to take my breath away," he said.

"Baby, I feel that God made you for me. You know just what to say. I love you," I said.

He reached his hand across the center console and grabbed my hand, lifted it to his face, and kissed it. "Thank you for having me as your husband."

In addition to being rugged, strong, and in charge, Jacob has a gentle side. I love it all about him.

I had booked the back room at Evons, a privately owned restaurant in the heart of downtown. His employees and their spouses or dates trickled into the room. Jacob was charming, dashing, and entertaining as usual. During the entire evening, he would wink at me from across the room, brush up next to me, and make growling sounds. I'd smile, cock my head, and raise my eyebrows.

The evening was filled with good food, laughter, dancing, and friends. Jacob is very social even though he always tries to make an excuse to go to a function. He says that he is just a home guy. I see him as both. He can certainly be the life of the party as well as the nurturing dad. I love all aspects of him.

It's funny how emotions can sway so much. At this time, I was so content and happy. The mundane chores, cooking meals, and driving a taxi for the kids didn't matter. I would have never considered conjuring up a plan to seduce my husband. Here I go again—ready to not follow through again. Dare I? Life was so good with Jacob. I didn't need to seduce him. He already loves me.

What do I do? I thought.

CHAPTER 6

Phase Two

The next day, when I picked the kids up from Annie's, Jill wanted to know all about the party. Michael wasn't interested, but he listened because he was in the car. I told them how handsome Daddy looked, how everyone enjoyed their gifts, and how good the food was. She asked several detail questions to which Michael had to listen to the answers.

We also decided that we would have a game night. Jacob didn't really enjoy games, but when he received three puppy dog faces, he sat down at the table too. We played Yahtzee. When we finished several games, Jacob started to see if he could throw the dice in the cup. That ended up being a competition. It was kind of like *horse* in basketball. We played for a while, then I sent the kids off to get ready for bed. It was a fun family night.

Once they were tucked in, I grabbed my planning notebook from my dresser. Jacob was vegging with an old Western movie. I decided that I was not going to quit on my plan. It was a go. I scribbled on the paper: "Dear Jacob."

Okay, I sat for a moment to think about my wording. I didn't want to come on too strong with the first letter but also wanted to pique his interest. The words came spilling out of my head, and I wrote quickly. I stopped and read it. I just wanted to get his attention with this. I would type and print it in the morning.

Jacob was so involved with the old Western, and I felt tired from the late evening yesterday. I walked over and kissed him tenderly on the forehead.

"I don't know why you love me so much, but I sure am happy," he said.

"Because you were made for me," I answered. "I love you."

I still had to figure out how I was going to deliver the notes without being detected. I could go to his office in the morning and put it on his desk. No one would be working because of New Year.

So in the morning, I would run out for donuts and swing by the office before returning home. At that point, there would definitely be no turning back.

I laid my head down and drifted into deep slumber thinking about the blessings in my life, a loving, hardworking, devoted husband; two sweet, kind children; a welcoming home; health; family; and friends. It was going to be a happy New Year!

Everyone was still in slumber land when I woke. I went to my computer and typed my first secret love letter.

Dear Jacob,

You are truly a remarkable man, and you really impress me. I have been able to see you take care of business with such ease and confidence and just handle life so well.

You are so kind and caring. It is evident with everyone you meet. You interact as if everyone is a longtime friend. From young to old, you know how to make everyone feel important.

You always make me feel special. I cherish every moment that I can be close to you. All men should be like you.

Your secret admirer

I checked for mistakes, reread, inserted the turquoise paper, and hit print. Short and sweet—not too mushy—but not too vague. I hope it gets him thinking. I signed it, "Your secret admirer" with my turquoise pen, disguised my signature to match the previous "Jacob"

I wrote on the envelopes, folded it, and put it in the envelope. One final touch was to add the puzzle pieces. I took the envelope labeled January 2 and inserted those pieces into the *love note*, sealed it, and slid it into my purse.

Everyone was still asleep or at least not up. I quickly got dressed, grabbed my purse, and headed out the door. I drove to the office first and put the envelope on his computer keyboard, smiled, and exited like a thief. I got back in my car and couldn't help but smile again. I couldn't believe that I was actually following through with my plan. My stomach was a little jittery. I felt like I was having a teenage crush.

I drove to get donuts, a rare treat. I selected everyone's favorites and drove home. The whole trip was under thirty minutes, and I could hear movement from across the house when I walked in the door. I turned on a fresh pot of coffee, and within minutes, everyone appeared in the kitchen. The kids were excited over the donuts as we all sat around the kitchen table. It was a nice way to enjoy the last day of the year.

CHAPTER 7

Reaction

I was on pins and needles all day, wondering, *When did Jacob find the letter? How did he react? Who did he think his secret admirer was? When was he coming home? Was he flattered?* My mind kept racing, and it was hard to concentrate on work as we all returned to school or work. I wanted to see him, to study his face. *Did I stump him? Did I intrigue him? Would he mention it to me? Did I make a mistake?* My mind was racing.

I tried my best to concentrate on work, but the library was not busy after the holiday. Most schools had resumed for the second semester. Over the past few years, there has been a shift in checking out books. Devices and apps have changed the way people read. We enticed people into the library through theatrics. I was working on finalizing our Valentine-themed program. About five years ago, I was approved to create monthly activities to bring in visitors. It has been quite successful. But like I said, my mind kept drifting.

I usually left work around two thirty to pick up the kids from school. Jill and Michael were chatter boxes when they entered the car. I welcomed their enthusiasm as it was a distraction from my own thoughts. They were thrilled to see and laugh with their friends. They talked all the way home, sometimes simultaneously. A warm feeling of comfort wrapped over me knowing that our children were happy, and so was I.

I started preparing dinner as soon as we arrived home—taco salad—a favorite for our family. It seemed as if the kids crashed as soon as they entered the house. Once back to a routine schedule plus concentration and excitement of the day, they decompressed in front of the TV. Their teachers kept homework minimal as they must have known their students' exhaustion level on their first day back.

Jacob drove into the driveway at about six, and my stomach did a little tumble. I tried to hold back my curiosity, but I wanted to blurt out every question in my head. I took a slow deep breath and turned toward the sink just before he entered the door. He walked up behind me and kissed the left side of my neck. I squeezed up my shoulder, turned, and kissed him. Trying not to be too inquisitive, I said, "Hi, babe. The kids had a great first day. How was your day?"

"Busy," he responded. Then Michael entered the kitchen and started spilling out facts about his day. *What?* I thought. *What about the note?* I couldn't blurt that out! I had to be patient. Jill came in a few minutes later, so I started to put the food on the table to eat. Jacob said that he would be right back as he wanted to change his clothes and wash his hands before we ate. We enjoyed dinner with lots of stories, giggles, and excitement from the kids.

After dinner, the minutes filled with clearing the plates, storing leftovers, washing dishes, and cleaning the table. Jacob told Michael to hit the shower and get ready for bed. It makes it easier to do this during the winter months when it gets dark so early. He didn't even object. I think he felt his own fatigue. Jill went to shower without even being told.

When I finished up in the kitchen, I joined Jacob in the family room where he was looking over some work papers. "It looks like your busy day isn't over," I casually said.

"A new client came in this morning with a big project. I'm excited to get him an estimate and options," he said. I thought I could approach more of a conversation, but Michael walked in. He sat down next to me, so he could do his reading assignment. He had grown so much with his reading skills, and he loved the challenge. When he finished, he ran off to get his homework sheet, so I could sign it. Jill, on the other hand, had her face buried in a book since she finished her shower. They both were exhausted, so we went in to pray with them and say good night. I love our *good-night routine.*

When we returned to the family room, I asked Jacob to tell me about his new project. He started to spew all sorts of details, sizes, styles, materials, and costs, but then he switched and said, "With all that going on, I also have a secret admirer."

I cocked my head to the right and lowered my left eye as I voiced, "Did you say 'secret admirer'?"

"I sure did. I received a note from someone who thinks I'm wonderful. Somebody wants me, baby." He proudly stated.

"Tell me more," I sounded intrigued.

"When I got to work this morning, there was an envelope sitting on my desk. I was curious, so I opened it. I wonder if it's from Becky, but she started dating a guy. I meant to bring it home, but things got so busy. Basically, it said that I am an awesome guy. So you better watch out."

I stood up, walked over to him, took his hand, and led him to the bedroom. "Well, why don't you show me how awesome you are?" I teased.

CHAPTER 8

Sexy Dad

For mid-January, I planned my next love note. You know how you always hear women say they like it when a man dotes on his children? Well, I took that approach in my next letter.

Dear Jacob,

> You are an amazing dad. I think it is cute how you pull out your phone and show off your children. I feel the pride and love you have for them. I know you are active and involved in their lives. You are an encourager and allow their minds to be curious. You are a great role model not only for your children but also for your employees and clients. Your natural common sense, decisive attitude, and guidance help so many people. Your nurturing demeanor helps so many of us. I find all these qualities to add up to be appealing—yes, you are one sexy dad.
>
> So captivated,
> Your secret admirer

Fourteen-plus years with this man, and life with him was so good. I find my husband the sexy dad to our children. Yes, he is handsome, but he also provides for our family, is a faithful servant to God, cares about others, and is genuine to the core—and he is mine.

I typed the letter when I got home with the kids from school. I rechecked it twice while the kids tackled their homework. I quickly took my paper stash, printed it, signed it (in my incognito signature), and added the puzzle pieces. At that point, I realized that Jacob had not mentioned the puzzle pieces with the first letter. I hope he didn't throw them away. Did he realize they had significance? I wondered what he did with them. He never brought the letter home, and I didn't want to pursue it as it might cause suspicion. I slid the envelope into my purse.

I delivered the note the next morning before I went to work. No one was at the office yet, so the timing was perfect. I inserted it in the keys on his computer just like last time to stay consistent.

Again, I felt like a teenager with a schoolgirl crush as I drove to work with a smile that spread across my face. I couldn't believe that I was actually continuing with my plan. This was good.

When Jacob pulled into the garage that evening, butterflies erupted in my stomach. I tried my best to act nonchalant. I walked toward him, kissed him, and asked him if he had a good day.

I barely finished when he blurted, "Well, baby, I definitely have a secret admirer. I received another letter, this time telling me that I am one sexy dad. So you better watch out. Somebody wants me, baby!

"Oh, really. Well, I'll try my best." I tried to make light of it.

He added, "Both of the letters had puzzle pieces in them. What do you suppose that means?"

"Puzzle pieces of what?" I asked inquisitively.

"I'm not really sure. But my guess would mean that more notes are coming. Maybe it will make a whole puzzle. Right now, they are just part of the outer edge. Nothing of significance, but I'm sure there is a purpose for it," he said. "Anyway, I'm intrigued."

"Well, so am I. Do you have any idea who is sending them? How are they addressed?" I asked.

"They aren't coming through the mail. They appeared on my desk, so I am thinking that it has to be someone tied to work.

The kids came into the kitchen exclaiming how famished they were. Because it was a cold winter day, I made a pot of turkey chili. Jill quickly set the table, Jacob said the blessings, and our tastebuds were satisfied. Giggles and stories filled the in-between moments. I really cherish these family moments.

CHAPTER 9

Determined

One thing I really love about Jacob was his drive. He always told me that before he met me, he could have cared less about his future. He was content to live in the moment without a plan. Don't get me wrong; he wasn't frivolous or irresponsible. I don't think those words would ever describe him. But he said that he didn't have a purpose. I was his purpose. He was determined to be a good provider. He was determined to make a good life for us. He was determined to be a good dad. He was determined to have a successful business. He was determined to treat others with respect and kindness. This list could go on and on. That always makes me smile. So it only made sense that my next love letter should center around that—it was a quality that everyone observed.

It was the first week of February when I started my third *anonymous* letter.

Dear Jacob,

Your drive and determination are so refreshing in a world where these qualities are being replaced with laziness and entitlement. A hardworking man with goals and plans is so appealing. Not only do you apply these qualities to work, which is totally evident to your clients and employees, but it is apparent in other aspects of

your life. I see these as part of your health con-
sciousness. You are fit, an impressive specimen of
a man I dare say. You always look so yummy.

Any woman would love to be seen on your
arm. I know I would.

Longingly,
Your secret admirer

I know I was not a seductive girl, I was naïve, and I didn't know
how to talk *dirty*. I didn't know what actually attracts a man, but I
did my best.

On Saturday morning, I typed the letter while everyone was
still sleeping. I wouldn't be able to print it because the paper was in
my dresser, and Jacob was still asleep. I just finished when Michael
appeared in the family room.

He asked if he could have pancakes for breakfast, so we headed
to the kitchen. He wanted to actually do it himself, so I guided him
through everything. Jill entered the room just as he was about to
put them on his plate. Jacob wasn't too far behind. He came up
behind me and wrapped his arms around my waist, kissed the back
of my neck, and said, "I know what I'm having for breakfast!" After
a long pause and raising his eyebrows up and down at me, he stated,
"Pancakes!" Michael may have wished that he didn't offer them to
everyone as he had to make another batch before he enjoyed the
fruits of his labor. Jacob showed him how to flip the pancake in the
air. He was quite the chef.

After breakfast, everyone headed to get ready for the day. I
headed to the bedroom; Jacob followed. He whispered, "I'm not quite
finished with breakfast." Okay, we may have taken a little longer to
shower and get dressed, but it was a lazy, winter Saturday morning.
Jacob helped me make the bed, and he exited the room with a wink.
I smiled.

Later that night, I printed the letter, added the puzzle pieces,
and put it all in the envelope. I delivered it on Monday morning
before work. I was determined to follow this plan to the end.

Jacob came home a little later than usual on Monday. He greeted me with a kiss and stated that his day was exhausting but then he added, "But when you are being blessed with a growing business, you can't complain."

There was no mention of the letter until the kids shuffled off to bed. That was when he sat down, elevated his feet, and told me that he received another special note. "I'm telling you, baby, this woman is coming onto me. The puzzle pieces were in there, but I still don't know who it is. Do you think she knows I am married?"

CHAPTER 10

My Valentine

I loved the excitement that writing the letters gave me. I was in a rut and needed some spice. At some weddings, a bag of salt is given as a symbol to add flavor to a marriage. That was my purpose—to add flavor. I was concentrating on all the wonderful characteristics of Jacob, not the burdensome chores. Our relationship was growing stronger. I didn't seem to mind the laundry, cooking, cleaning, running errands, taxiing children, and the rest.

Jacob was my Valentine—always was and always will be. I didn't want to give him a letter for Valentine's Day because I wanted his concentration to be totally about me, even though the letters were from me. I hope that makes sense.

I had a love theme all set up for the library. I had signs made with the look of conversational heart candy. I had volunteers who dressed as the characters in their favorite love story book. There was a kissing booth with puppies from the animal shelter. The puppies were all available for adoption. Heart-shaped cookies were passed out. The noise was a little louder than normal because of it, but everyone enjoyed themselves. Volunteer readers shared books with the children in animated dramatics. I spent so much time organizing all the activities that I had little time to concentrate on my love notes.

I also volunteered to send items to the school for Valentine's parties for both Jill and Michael. I didn't know what I was thinking. I wanted to be able to assist at their parties, but the library festivities took all my time.

The 14th landed on a Thursday this year, so I was looking forward to Friday when everything settled down. Jacob asked me if I wanted to go out on Saturday for a romantic dinner. We really enjoyed making special moments rather than buying *stuff* for each other. I was so happy that we didn't feel obligated to buy gifts just because society deemed it a special day. Annie and I made arrangements to watch each other's children. I was on duty on Friday, and she took Saturday. I knew I looked forward to Friday, but her kids were easy. We played a few board games and chilled with popcorn or a movie.

Saturday morning was lazy as the kids didn't stir until almost nine. It was nice to have coffee in bed among other things. Annie came at about eleven to pick up the kids. I spent the next three hours cleaning and doing laundry. I didn't mind any of it.

Jill and Michael were tired from the later night. We planned to pick them up at about nine thirty instead of letting them sleep over. After all, they did have school on Monday, and I didn't want their schedules to be too far off.

At five, Jacob showered and I was right behind him. He dressed and left the room while I was still showering. I put on a short red dress and heels. When I walked through the family room, Jacob, with eyebrows raised said, "Wow!" He walked closer looking mighty dapper in a suit and open-necked white shirt. He hated wearing a tie, but he sure looked amazing and smelled yummy. He leaned in close and whispered in my ear, "Baby, you still wow me!"

I smiled and said, "You still catch my eye too!" Then he kissed me passionately. The kids made some disgusting noises, but Jill added, "You should go out more often. You both look so nice."

Annie only lived about two miles from us. We drove the kids there and returned home, and we both decided that Valentine's was the perfect day for love. Our reservation wasn't until seven fifteen, which we just made it.

CHAPTER 11

Continue

My whole purpose for writing the letters was to spice up our marriage—to add a little excitement. I don't know if it was the letters or my attitude that caused this paradigm shift. I was loving our relationship. It always was good, but now it was great—not just our sex life but admiration for each other. Was it because I was more appreciative? Was it that I was an active participant in a game? I didn't know. So should I continue with the letters? I kept debating about it but kept thinking about being a quitter. About two weeks later, I pulled out my laptop and wrote another letter. I was off my schedule that I made, but I could combine some ideas.

Dear Jacob,

I love your witty responses. You always know when and how to lighten the mood. From casual conversations to intense issues, you know how to keep the atmosphere appropriate and enjoyable. I've heard you deliver a punchline causing the entire room to chuckle and roar with laughter. I'm sure you can deliver a whole lot more.

I've enjoyed the times that I have been in your presence—you lighten the room, but you make me feel like I'm on a cloud. Your smile, humor, and laugh are so sexy.

Wishing more,
Your secret admirer

Everyone was busy with projects of their own. Jacob was working on locating a specific item his client wanted to incorporate into the design. Jill was reading in her bedroom, and Michael was buried in Legos. I slipped off to get my paper and print this letter. I found my puzzle pieces and dropped them in the pre-addressed envelope as well. I delivered that one on a Wednesday morning, the first week of March. I still couldn't wait to hear his reaction. Butterflies still filled my stomach thinking about it.

That evening when Jacob arrived home, I was putting a load of laundry into the washer. He came up behind me, put his arms around my waist, and kissed the side of my neck. I jumped and let out a little squeal. I don't know why I was surprised. I guess I was deep in thought and didn't hear him. I quickly turned around and put my arms around his neck and kissed him. He said, "Hope your day was good. I smell the roast. I'm going to change. I'm starved." Then he left the room with a flourish.

He didn't say anything else. I wanted to follow him to the bedroom but didn't want to raise suspicion. I walked to the kitchen and called Jill and Michael to dinner. Jacob followed, blessed the food, and started talking to the kids about school. Jill mentioned that she had a note about a bookfair. That's when Jacob winked at me and said that he received a note too. He caught me off guard, and I almost said, "I was wondering if you were going to mention it." I caught myself and said, "A note?" in an inquisitive voice.

Jacob answered, "Yes, just telling me that I have a great sense of humor."

"You are funny, Dad! I want to be like that," Michael chirped in. And before you knew it, the corny jokes began, and the note conversation stopped. I wanted to know his reaction, his feelings, and his curiosity level, but all I received was, "Why is six afraid of seven? Because seven ate nine!"

And that was the end of any conversation about the note he received.

CHAPTER 12

Wishful Thinking

Jacob was so attentive and loving. Often he would wrap his arms around me and say, "I don't deserve you," or "I'm glad you love me so much!" I believe that throughout each year, everyone has ups and downs. We have to talk our way through because if not, we hang in the *down* parts and never get to celebrate the *up* parts. Positive thinking and finding the joys around us make life more interesting and fun. I wish that when we start thinking that we are victims, we change that thought and think of ourselves as victors.

I was in a *down* spot when I first started my *secret admirer* adventure. Now I didn't need the spice, but for some reason, I didn't want to quit. Again, I think it is because I wanted to run the whole race because I already had so much time invested in it.

I love that it gave me motivation and purpose to lose weight which will always boost my self-esteem. I love that it led me on a road that made me appreciate my life and family. I love that all the optimism flooded our home.

So I continued to write to Jacob. It was the end of March, and I pulled out my laptop and wrote:

Dear Jacob,

How can you be so nurturing to so many people? You are always strategic and calm—the perfect balance. I cherish a guy who can deliver so much in a relationship.

Everyone can count on you. When you say, "I will handle it," you do! You are so dependable—again—a rare quality and one that is so desirable. You are the type of man that any woman would admire and hold dear.

Jacob, you are a very desirable man. As I watch you from a distance, I wish the space between us would lessen. I get chills thinking of drawing closer. That thought gives me comfort, arousal, warmth, and joy. You could hold me anytime, and I would cherish the moment.

Wishful thinking,
Your secret admirer

The kids were riding their bikes in the driveway with some neighborhood friends, and Jacob wasn't home, so I retrieved my paper. After rereading it once again, I printed it. Then I added a heart next to his name on the front of the turquoise envelope and inserted the puzzle pieces.

I began to wonder what intrigued him the most, the letter or the puzzle. He was so busy at work, and his mind did not stop when he was home. He was always obtaining prices and styles and searching for the perfect pieces for his clients. Often he asked me for my opinion or help. He knew that I loved decorating so if the client wasn't interested in making the choices, I would make selections and create a demo board for them.

When Jacob arrived home, he stayed outside with the kids. I got the meal on the table and called everyone inside. Jacob kissed me, and Michael made kissy sounds. That's when we both grabbed the kids and smothered them with kisses. Giggles filled the room with gasps from laughter. I absolutely love these moments. Parenthood is worth every moment.

Again I delivered it the next morning, a Tuesday. The thoughts of his reaction filled my mind throughout the day, bringing a smile. I felt mischievous but not wild.

CHAPTER 13

What Changed

Jacob came home at about six. Jill was sitting at the kitchen table, and Michael and I were working on his spelling words in the family room. He kissed Jill on the top of her head then came to kiss me and ruffle Michael's hair. "How was everyone's day?" he cheerfully asked.

Jill was thrilled to tell him that she had a lead part in her grade-level show. She was not afraid to perform as her confidence level was high. Additional practices were needed on her part so she would have to stay for an extra hour at school on Tuesdays and Thursdays for the month of April. Her schedule was tight as she had dance on Monday after school, and Wednesday evening was church.

Michael had T-ball practice on Monday and Thursday from six to seven. The balancing scale was in full force. Our connections with classmates' parents helped with carpooling and taxiing.

We ate dinner with continuous talk about all the activities. Then Jacob and Michael headed outside to practice hitting the baseball. They didn't last long as it was getting too dark. That was followed by showers and a little TV. Jacob had not mentioned the note. Would he wait for the kids to go to bed?

Once they were asleep, Jacob turned on the news and relaxed—still no comment on the note. I wanted to mention work, but when I looked at him, his eyes were closed. Spring weather ignites projects which means more business for Jacob. He was exhausted.

I felt let down. I loved his reactions to the letters. I read for a while nestled on the edge of the couch, but I soon got drowsy. I kissed him on his forehead and went to bed. He barely budged.

The next morning, I woke, showered, and made the coffee. I woke the kids and then took Jacob a cup of coffee. It was our normal routine. Jacob said, "Thanks, babe. I'm sorry I crashed last night. I have been so busy at work. After such a delicious meal, I just mellowed."

"I understand, hun. If there is anything I can do to help, just let me know," I said.

"Well, there is one thing…" he said as he pulled me onto the bed.

"Sorry. Kids are up, and I have to get ready for work, *and* so do you." I tried to sound stern.

"Then later." He raised his eyebrows as he spoke.

Jill called me from her room. As I exited, I said, "Yes, later!" Jill wanted me to French braid her hair. When I finished that, I headed to the kitchen to make breakfast. Jacob was getting a second cup of coffee, and I headed to get dressed. We were on autopilot for getting ready, and we had to leave. There was no time to talk.

I kissed everyone goodbye and headed out the door. As I drove to work, I wondered, *Why didn't he mention the letter?* I made an excuse for him. He was tired and fell asleep. He would mention it this evening.

But that evening, he didn't say anything about his secret admirer—not a word. The past times, he mentioned it the same day, and then he subtly brought it up several times in the weeks to come. Like he would say, "Do you want this sexy dad?" or "I can make an impression on you if you let me." Or "My plans include you after the kids go to bed." Each comment matched up to the letters sent. So what changed with this one?

He didn't talk about it at all. Not that day or the days to follow. What changed? I was curious but didn't know how to bring up the conversation. I decided to wait until the next one.

CHAPTER 14

Anticipated Reaction

My mind had to concentrate on so many things—kids, work, demonstration boards, taxiing, and my plan (of which I was off my schedule). I kept thinking about why Jacob gave no reaction to the last love letter. I pulled out my laptop and reread the last one given. Could anything have been misconstrued? Was it boring? I felt like I was faltering in my plan. Since I had my computer out, I started another one. I would deliver it in the morning.

Dearest Jacob,

I imagine life to be so adventurous and fun with you. You are always eager to try new skills or challenges. I've watched you participate in so many activities. Your skills are plentiful as you are strong, muscular, and agile. It is evident even in your walk. I love it when you walk toward me— or away. That view is equally appealing.

That can-do attitude opens new possibilities for new experiences. I'd love to share them with you.

Your new experience,
Your secret admirer

Surely, he would mention this one. I had a few minutes before I had to pick up Jill and her classmate, Maggie, from practice. Michael was outside with the neighborhood children playing T-ball. I collected all my necessary items—paper, marker, envelope, and puzzle pieces. I quickly put the paper in the printer and hit *print*. I felt my confidence return when I completed my process and inserted the puzzle pieces. It was time to leave. I put the envelope in my purse.

Michael said, "Goodbye," to his friends, and climbed in the backseat. As we were driving out of the driveway, I saw Jacob's truck at the end of the road. Michael asked if he could stay home with him. He jumped out of the car at the end of the driveway.

I pulled out of the driveway and rolled down my window. Jacob stopped next to me so our windows were facing each other. I said, "I'm headed to pick up Jill. Michael's all yours."

"And I'm all yours!" he said winking his eye. "See you in a bit." It's with comments like that that I knew everything was all right. He was just busy with work, I kept telling myself.

I drove past his office on the way to get the girls. It looked like everyone had gone home, so I slipped into his office and put the envelope on his keyboard as usual.

I arrived with not a minute to spare to pick up the girls from practice. After dropping Maggie off, Jill and I headed home. We talked about her practice. Mixed feelings began to develop as her performance date came closer. She shared how she was happy with her part and participating but anxious about the whole thing. Because I could relate, I was able to calm her nervousness as well as my own. I was executing my plan, and hopefully, it wouldn't fail.

CHAPTER 15

Glimmer

But is it failing? Jacob came home from work the following day with no comment at all about his secret admirer or the content of the letter. Jill and Michael were completing their homework, and I was setting the table. The house was filled with saucy smells of stuffed shells and garlic. The salad anchored the center of the table. Jacob set his work stuff on the end of the counter, wrapped his arms around me, and announced, "Honey, I'm home." Then he kissed me.

"So how was your day?" I quickly asked, hoping for information about the letter.

"Well, we are wrapping up one project, juggling three more, and initiating another one. God has been so good to us," he joyfully stated.

How could I follow that with "I am your temptress. Why haven't you mentioned me?" I wanted to straight out ask him if he had received any new advances from his secret admirer, but that would have exposed the plan. It was not the right timing.

After dinner, everyone helped with the cleanup. Then we played Scrabble before the kids went to bed. There wouldn't be many more days for board games as the weather was getting too nice to remain inside. At the end of the game, Jacob said, "Let's go hiking this Saturday. We can pack some sandwiches and include a picnic. We've all been working hard, and we can use a break before Michael's games start next week. Let's be adventurous." Was that a reference to the love letter? Maybe. How would I know?

There was a glimmer of hope that my plan was still working.

We woke at six thirty on Saturday morning and got dressed, and everyone grabbed a quick breakfast of their choice. We added ice and drinks to the cooler and loaded the car by seven. We drove north for two hours to get to Hieroglyphic Trails. The trail would be easy for the kids. We had so much fun driving and walking the trails, giggling, and having science and history lessons from Professor Dad. A little over an hour into the hike, Jacob explained about the rock carvings called petroglyphs. When we continued on the trail, he grabbed my hand and laid a flat rock in it, and said, "My petroglyph for you." He had carved "My eyes R 4 U." (For the word *eyes*, he actually drew eyes.) Then he leaned in and kissed me. My heart melted. He had planned the whole adventure.

My love for my husband keeps growing. We continued our hike holding hands. We saw cacti in bloom and tried to name all the wildflowers that led to the canyon. Boulders filled the area. We saw pools of water but no waterfall. We would have to time that closer to rain. Jill and Michael climbed rocks, explored, and enjoyed the fresh air.

Jacob was the perfect dad and husband. That evening after the kids crashed, he took my hand and said, "I have one more trail for you to follow." It's these moments that I am glad that I started the whole puzzle romance.

CHAPTER 16

Continued Plan

With no discussion of the letters for three weeks, I debated whether I should continue the plan. I thought he would need closure for the love interest, so I decided to continue my scheme.

On Thursday, I stopped and picked barbeque for dinner. It made the evening a little smoother because of the kids' schedules. Next Thursday evening was Jill's performance at the school, so life would soon get a little easier. Since I didn't have to cook, I pulled out my laptop and wrote:

Dearest Jacob,

You are such a great balance—rugged yet tender, affectionate, and kind. I've seen you with children, patiently giving help, teaching, and instilling values. I've seen you with adults, giving advice and encouragement. You know how to react with composure and thought. I've heard stories of when you offered assistance to strangers, laid the money down when someone was short of cash, and did work for someone without charging.

Your compassion for others is such an attractive quality. You think of others and genuinely want them to succeed and be well. I find your personality so appealing. I know that I desire you.

Hopeful,
Your secret admirer

I followed my routine, printing, adding the puzzle pieces, and placing them in my purse. I stopped by the office on my way to pick up Jill and dropped it off. I sat parked on the street as one car was still in the parking lot. I had a few minutes to spare. Just as I was about to drive off, Claire, the cleaning lady emerged from the building. She got in her car and drove off.

I pulled up next to the building, unlocked the door, entered the alarm code, and went to Jacob's office. I put the envelope on his keyboard. The next love letter was placed. Excitement filled my mind again.

CHAPTER 17

Deflated

I woke with excitement about Jacob's predicted reaction this time. I just knew that he would come home and say, "I'm really a prize catch you know—at least my secret admirer thinks so." When he arrived home, I felt my stomach tumble as we were outside enjoying the fresh spring weather. He laid his case on the car hood and joined us. I casually said, "Hi, babe. Did you have a good day?"

"It was a full day. I spent most of my time on the job sites. Everything is on schedule or ahead. Keep your eye on the ball, Michael," he said as he threw him a pitch. His purpose shifted to giving pointers to Michael. I walked toward Jill who was in the outfield. She took left. I took right. It was nice to be outside.

After about thirty minutes, I headed inside to get dinner on the table. "Don't be long," I said. They followed me inside. Jacob picked up his binder case and walked into the house with the kids at his heels. "Wash up, everyone." They all headed to their rooms. Jacob appeared in the kitchen with a T-shirt and jersey shorts. He kissed me on the cheek as I put the salad on the table. "Good day?" he asked.

"Nothing out of the ordinary," I said hoping to jog his mind. "Just a normal day."

I was expecting him to have at least some reference to receiving another love note, but there was no mention of it that evening. I kept playing different scenarios in my mind as to why he didn't say anything. I kept thinking that he would be flattered and would want to share it with me.

I was deflated. That was twice that he didn't bring up the subject of being the object of someone's desires. I spent so much time and energy playing my game, but I clearly was not the winner. What was he thinking? Was he curious about who it was? Did he initiate a conversation with someone whom he thought it was?

A week had passed and still no response about receiving a love note. I tried to initiate the conversation with "Anything interesting going on at work?" "Any new clients?" Whatever tactic I tried failed. Without directly asking him, I would not get a response.

My mind was racing with *what-ifs*. What if he was actively pursuing conversations with women thinking it might be them? What if his curiosity had piqued his interest in other women? What if I was not that exciting to him? I started to question my motives. Do I continue? I found myself being mad at him—how crazy. I was the one who began this whole enticement, yet I was upset that it didn't spark a reply. But how could it—he didn't know from where the letters were coming.

Thursday evening was Jill's program. She was nervous and excited. Jacob texted me to let me know that he would meet us at the school. He was running late. When he entered the auditorium, a group of mothers standing close to the entrance stopped him. They talked, laughed, and smiled. Oh, was I feeling jealous? Maybe. I have never been like that.

When he approached me, he grabbed Michael's head and made a twisting sound. Then he kissed me and said, "Sorry that I had to meet you rather than us coming together. Business is exploding. Some of the windows for the Mitchell's job were the wrong size, and I was trying to get them fixed. I don't want it to set the job behind."

Jill was fabulous with her parts and her singing. She looked confident and connected with the audience. Jacob reached over and held my hand, "I'm so proud of her."

We were in separate cars. Jill was with me, and Michael rode with Jacob. When we arrived home, I warmed Jacob's meal and pulled out the ice cream to celebrate. We sat at the table where Jacob and Michael shot one positive affirmation after another to Jill. She beamed and blushed at the same time. I love my family.

CHAPTER 18

Almost There

Another week and a half went by and still no mention of his admirer. He came home late three evenings that week because he met with clients. He was exhausted, and we barely saw each other. Was he involved with someone else? The thought of that made me sick to my stomach. Jacob is not like that. I kept telling myself, "He is faithful."

I just had one more letter before I sent the invitation. I had to talk myself into continuing. I wanted to drown my disillusions in food, but that wouldn't solve anything. I was the one who started this whole charade, so I might as well finish it. I was almost there.

I took my laptop in hand and began to type:

My Dear Jacob,

Every aspect of you is sexy—your walk, the way you turn your head slightly when you are deep in thought, your stance. I could make a giant list of what I find appealing. When you are close, I desire your voice, your breath, your touch. I want to make each day more enjoyable, interesting, fresh, and fun.

I can be more than a secret to you. I am your true admirer. I want to touch and hold you,

to share special moments, to press my lips against
yours, to feel your skin touch mine.
I want to be yours—forever.

Anticipating forever,
Your secret admirer

Surely that will pique his curiosity, I thought. I printed it, signed
it, and added the puzzle pieces. The envelope with the puzzle pieces
revealing my face was reserved for the invitation. I held the envelope,
staring at "Jacob" written on the front. I wished I could have climbed
into his mind. I wanted to know his thoughts. Did he anticipate
receiving the letters? Did he want to meet her/me?

I stopped by his office the next morning and delivered it.
Luckily, I arrived before everyone else. The crews didn't report to the
office before they went to the job sites. Jacob would often visit the
sites before he went in.

I was so involved in work, finishing up the touches for May's
special event that I barely thought about the note. My theme was centered around National Mother Goose Day and National Lemonade
Day. Every hour Mother Goose would read a nursery rhyme and
characters acted it out.

Jacob surprised me around eleven thirty with chicken salad and
fresh fruit from Mammy's, my favorite local restaurant. He knew that
I wouldn't get a break from the festivities to eat lunch, so he figured
that I might be able to grab a nibble throughout the day. As he leaned
in to kiss me goodbye, he whispered, "You can rub-a-dub-dub in my
tub any day." I giggled out loud. The thought of my love note never
crossed my mind until after he left.

When I picked the kids up from school, they wanted to know
about the rhymes chosen. All the way home we sang and chanted
"Mary Had a Little Lamb," "Baa Baa Black Sheep," "Humpty
Dumpty," and many others and acted plain silly. The whole day was
fun and whimsical.

Jacob arrived around six. We were outside in the fresh air and
sunshine. I love springtime—the shades popping out, fragrances that

fill the air, and new beginnings. Michael ran toward him with a baseball in hand and asked for some pitches. Jill and I took our places in the outfield. We stayed out for about thirty minutes when I said, "We better eat."

"One of the suppliers is sending lunch to the office for everyone tomorrow. If you can slip out, you should come. The food is being delivered at noon," Jacob said. I thought that would be fun. I rarely leave the library throughout the day, but it should be a quiet day since yesterday was so eventful. Maybe I could ask his employees some innocent questions.

Again, he didn't mention his secret admirer. Why? I was so frustrated with his nonreaction. The entire evening, Jacob did not mention one word. My disappointment kept multiplying. Jill and Michael sensed something was bothering me. I told them that I had a headache that I couldn't shake. I reassured them that I would be all right after a good night's sleep.

After the kids went to bed, Jacob came up behind me as I stood at the bathroom sink and started rubbing my neck and shoulders very gently but firmly. "Do you think I can make your headache disappear?" he softly whispered in my ear. I wanted to be mad, but then I pictured him bringing me lunch and I melted. I turned and kissed him and said, "You are my knight in shining armor—rescued me at lunch and now!"

That was my reassurance that he was faithful. Our sex life was healthy and strong. If he showed a love interest in someone else, I would expect our relationship to diminish, but it was consistent and more than just sex. We connected with each other on a deeper level.

The next morning, I put extra thought into my outfit. What if I had competition? I wanted to look my best. Why was I thinking like that? What if he took extra notice of the women with whom he interacted? What if…? I had so many thoughts swimming around in my head. I didn't like the way I felt or thought. I was the one that initiated this whole scheme. Jacob was innocent, yet I was mad that he kept the notes from me. He should have shared them. Why was he hiding them? How could he do this to me?

CHAPTER 19

Investigation

The next day I slipped away from the library leaving two trusty employees, Ann and Marie, to handle the patrons and visitors. Since I rarely left during open hours, they encouraged me to go have lunch with my husband. I arrived at Jacob's office a few minutes after twelve. I hadn't anticipated the amount of lunch traffic on the roads. When I entered, Jacob had his back toward the door, but he turned around quickly when everyone shouted my name. He quickly scooted over to me, put his right arm around my waist, and kissed me. With excitement in his voice, he said, "I'm so glad that you were able to make it."

His reaction had always been the same when he saw me. From the time we met, he greeted me like I was the best surprise of his day, especially if we were away from home. He always made me feel special. While others were trying to greet me, he ushered me to the food table and asked me what I wanted. I placed a turkey and cheese croissant on the plate and some fresh pineapple and strawberries. He picked up a napkin and a fork and handed them to me. "I'll get you some tea," he said.

I walked over to the guys who were sitting in some temporary folding chairs that were randomly set around a folding table. I said, "Hi, guys! Is Jacob treating you right?"

"Always!" shouted Ray, one of the job foremen.

"We couldn't ask for better," said Ed through a half-packed mouth. I sat down in an empty chair.

I quickly added in a questioning voice, "So he's keeping on the straight and narrow?" I paused. "Nothing I need to worry about then?"

"You bet. Jake's the best." Mark blurted. For some reason, he always calls Jacob, Jake. It has even rubbed off on some of the other guys.

Jacob walked over and handed me some tea. He said, "I have to get some more ice. I'll be back in a bit." And off he went.

So I boldly asked, "Do you know anything about Jacob's secret admirer?"

"Oh, yeah. He was pretty pumped when he got his first letter, but it's been a while since he said anything. I don't think he is taking it seriously. He thinks we are playing a joke on him," said Ed.

"Is he still receiving them?" asked Mark.

Not wanting to sound totally knowledgeable and nodding my head slightly up and down, I said, "I believe so."

Ray piped in. "You don't have to worry about it. Jake talks about you and the kids all the time. He really loves you. Besides everyone here is taken—just in case you were interested." Then he winked. Everyone chuckled.

Jacob came back and pulled up a chair next to me. Everyone chitchatted for a few more minutes. I stood and said that I had to get back to the library but that I enjoyed their company so much. I bent over and kissed Jacob. He stood and walked me out to my car.

He opened my door, and I slid into my seat. "I love you, babe," he said. Then he leaned in and planted a big one on me.

"I love you too—enjoy your afternoon. Bye," I said. I drove to work with a smile on my face. Going for lunch really calmed my questioning mind. Nothing seemed out of sorts.

CHAPTER 20

The Invitation

At times during my wooing, I felt like I was cheating on Jacob. But I questioned if he had wandering eyes. This conflict existed within me, and I hated it. I was going to follow through with my plan as I was so close to the finish line. "All would be fine!" I kept reassuring myself.

I concentrated on so many other things that I almost forgot about our anniversary. We rarely bought each other gifts, but for some reason, I felt that this year I wanted to give him something special. I looked up the gifts given for the fifteenth anniversary. The traditional gift was crystal. It was to represent the marriage relationship as being delicate yet sturdy. A good marriage provided clarity and transparency. Those words summed up the past years well.

Then I saw that the modern gift was a watch. This encompassed time—past, present, and future. I liked that idea. I decided that a watch would be the perfect gift. I had been putting a little nest egg away for a few years, so I could make a purchase without him noticing.

I called my jeweler, Chuck, and told him what I wanted—a Rolex Sea Dweller. He said that it was a pretty good chunk of change. I knew it, but it was a special occasion. He said that he would have it for me on Saturday.

That evening after dinner, I worked on my last and final letter. Everyone was engaged with projects. Jacob was busy finalizing pricing for a client. Jill was working on a book report, and Michael was reading. We were all in the same space but focused on our individual goals.

Dear Jacob,

Every aspect of you is sexy and appealing to me. When I know you are close, I desire your voice, your touch, your wit, and more. I know you are content and happy, but I know that I can make those daily tasks even more enjoyable, interesting, fresh, and fun.

I want to be your true admirer, not just a secret one. One to touch and hold you, to share special moments, to press my lips to yours, to feel your skin touch mine. I want to be more than words on a page.

Please meet me at Marcos on Thursday, June 7 at 7:00.

My heart is yours,
Your secret admirer

I couldn't print it as everyone was present. I saved it and closed my laptop. Then I nestled next to Michael and had him read aloud. I asked Jill if she would like to go shopping with me on Saturday. She was excited.

When it was bedtime, I sat on the edge of her bed and softly told her that we were going to shop for an anniversary gift for Daddy. I told her to keep it a secret. Excitement filled her eyes as she smiled and shook her head up and down.

While Jacob was in with Michael as they were planning out their guy day for Saturday. I went to my dresser and took my final envelope with the puzzle pieces, pen, and paper. I slid it into my tote bag. I had to print it in the morning. In order for him to plan the meeting with (me), I had to deliver it in the morning. Then I headed into the bathroom to get ready for bed.

I walked back to the family room. Jacob was sitting in the club chair. As I walked past him, he grabbed my wrist. When I turned toward him, he held my other wrist and twirled me onto his lap. "This is where you belong," he said emphatically. "Let's go out to dinner next Saturday for our anniversary."

"Oh, you remembered," I said teasingly.

"After fifteen years with the same woman, I can't forget," he proudly said. "And I've enjoyed every moment."

I added, "I am happy to make them enjoyable." And with those words, he lifted me and carried me to the bedroom.

CHAPTER 21

Finale

After I finished getting ready for work, I took Jacob a cup of coffee and put it on his nightstand. Then I kissed him behind his ear as his back was toward the edge of the bed. I woke the kids and headed to my laptop. With my turquoise paper in hand, I loaded the printer and opened my document. I hit print. Michael came into the kitchen for breakfast. It was a cereal kind of morning as I was pressed for time. I took the paper from the printer, grabbed the marker from my tote, and mimicked "Your secret admirer." I folded it, inserted it into the marked envelope, and added the puzzle pieces. I quickly put it in my purse as I saw Jill walking in my direction. She reminded me that I needed to pick up some snacks for her field trip.

We walked to the kitchen. Michael was still eating, and Jill grabbed a pear and a breakfast bar. Jacob showed up a few minutes later with his empty coffee cup in hand. He poured himself another cup and sat at the table with Michael. "You better pick up the pace, kids."

That was my clue to get out the door. I gave kisses all around and said, "Enjoy your day! Love you all."

I drove directly to Jacob's office and placed the letter on his keyboard. I exited quickly as I didn't want to get caught. On my drive to work, I had mixed emotions about my adventure coming to an end—no more turquoise envelopes and no more love notes but also no more uncertainty.

I just knew that he would come home with excitement over receiving an invitation to meet his secret admirer as this was a *big* change from the previous notes. Then I would hand him the final pieces of the puzzle, but that is not how it happened.

Work felt long, and I was happy to pick up the kids. We stopped by the grocery store to pick up some items and snacks for Jill's field trip. I expected Jacob to text or call me when he opened the letter, but he didn't. He gets so busy, and he had a heavy load, right?

When he pulled into the driveway, those butterflies flew in all directions. He came walking through the door. "Hi, baby. Did you have a busy day?" I asked.

"Beyond busy!" he said. "I'm glad to be home, and I'm famished." We met each other midway in the kitchen and kissed each other. I wrapped my arms around him, squeezed him tight, then released him, patted his behind, and said, "Then go get cleaned up for dinner—it's ready."

He said, "Yes, ma'am."

Within a few minutes, everyone gathered in the kitchen. Jacob savored every bite of the meat loaf. "I didn't get a chance to eat lunch other than some grapes and coffee. It didn't last."

I asked, "What interesting things happened?" I just knew he was going to tell me about the invitation, but he had no mention of it or anything to do with his office. He only spoke about his guys and the job sites. Again my mind was questioning why. I didn't get to hand him the last puzzle pieces.

Around eleven on Saturday morning, Jill and I went shopping. We ran to a few of our favorite stores and then ate lunch. It was girl time. The guys left early for some fishing. After we ate lunch, we drove to the jewelers. When we walked in, he said, "I'm glad you waited until afternoon. The delivery arrived just a little while ago." He showed me how to set it. Jill was impressed and thought Daddy would love it. I paid Chuck, and we left.

When Jill and I arrived home, I took the watch and put it in my drawer next to the writing paper.

Jacob continued to make no reference to the letter at all. On Sunday evening, he said that he would be running late on Thursday. He was meeting someone about a proposition. So that's what he's calling it! He was going to go through with it. He was going to meet her—me. But he didn't know it was me. I was justified in being mad—right? I sat in the bedroom closet and cried. How could he!

Later I called Katie, the babysitter, and asked her if she could watch the kids on Thursday and Saturday nights. Luckily, she was free. Katie is a high school girl that lives about two blocks away. She is always willing to come. I told her that we might be late.

On Thursday, I took a half day off of work and headed to my hairdresser. When I arrived home, I pulled my secret black dress from the back of the closet and set out my jewelry and shoes. Then I sat outside to soak up some sunshine and pondered over the last months. I was so confused about this whole plan. Did I ruin my marriage with my puzzle antics? I totally enjoyed the thrill of the whole quest, the secret, the enticing thoughts, but at what cost? On the other hand, Jacob and I seemed closer than ever. But why hasn't he mentioned the love notes? Why did he make arrangements to meet his secret admirer? Curiosity? Attraction? Interest? I was making myself so confused thinking about it. What if everything backfired in my face?

It was almost time to pick the kids up from school. I went inside, showered, and put on my makeup. Then I drove to the school in yoga pants and a T-shirt. When Michael and Jill got in the car, she said, "Mom, you look so pretty! What are Daddy and you doing this evening? Where are you going?

I told them that it was our anniversary and that we were going to dinner. I didn't have to tell them to keep it a secret because Jacob wasn't returning home before he met his *meeting*. Then we talked about their school day.

When we arrived home, I sat with Michael as he read. Jill asked for some help with her math homework. Around six, I went to get ready. Jill came into my bathroom, zipped me up, and asked if I was giving Daddy the watch. I told her that I was saving that for Saturday. She stood by my side as I put on my jewelry and lipstick. I told her that when she was older that I hoped she met someone just like Daddy. The doorbell rang. Jill ran to get the door as I told her Katie was coming. I grabbed my shoes and headed to the kitchen.

"Wow, Mom! You look so pretty," said Michael. Katie turned her head toward me and said, "He's right!"

I left money for pizza delivery for Katie and the kids. I told Katie that I wasn't sure what time we would arrive home, but we would be in separate cars.

I kissed the kids goodbye, put on my shoes, grabbed my purse which contained the final puzzle pieces, and headed out the door. My thoughts were all over the place. What would I say to Jacob? How would I approach him? Would I be angry with him for meeting her (me)? How could he follow through with this invitation? As I drove to the restaurant, I felt sick to my stomach. How could I have done this to my beloved husband? I was blaming him, then me, then him—Why did I ever come up with this plot? What if he was interested in her? I kept playing scenarios in my mind. I pulled up to the restaurant and drove through the parking lot. Jacob's truck was parked on the right side of the building. There was an empty parking space close to him. I pulled in, parked, shut off the car, and sat for a minute saying a short prayer for a happy outcome. I took a couple of relaxing breaths and spoke out loud, "You started this. Now go finish it with a happy ending. You have this!" I opened the door and walked toward the entrance door. Confidentially, I walked inside.

CHAPTER 22

Content

The hostess looked directly at me, smiled, and asked, "How many?"

"I'm meeting someone here." I looked past her and could see Jacob's back of his head. As I lifted my head slightly in his direction, I said, "I see him. I want to surprise him." She nodded her head up and down.

He was wearing his black suit. I wondered when he took it out of the house. When he left this morning, he had on khakis and his logo business polo. He must really be trying to impress her. I was ready for anything. I stepped to the side, reached into my purse, pulled out the last few pieces of the puzzle, and arranged them in a stack in my right hand.

I tried to act confident as I walked with wobbly knees toward him. I just knew that my heart was about to be broken. *Why was he sitting with his back toward the door?* I thought. I would have been looking at the door for a woman to walk in. I walked up behind him, slid my left arm up his shoulder blade and rested it on his shoulder, leaned slightly forward, and laid the puzzle pieces on the table directly in front of him on the white tablecloth while holding my head back. He didn't even turn around. It seemed like a long moment before he spoke.

"Happy anniversary, baby," he spoke softly and confidently. What? That was not the reaction that I was expecting. I stepped back away from his chair. He slid his chair back slightly, rose from his chair, turned and looked at me, smiled, and said, "I've been waiting a long time to meet my secret admirer. And she is mighty fine." He took a step back, eyed me up and down, and drooled, "Um, um, you still take my breath away." Then he stepped in, slid his right arm around my waist, pulled me close to him, and kissed me.

"But how? How did you know it was me?" I stuttered inquisitively. I know that I didn't have to ask the question because it was written all over my face.

"Because I know you, honey." He pulled out a chair for me to sit on. I slid into the seat. "I know how you think. I know your semantics. I know your heart. I recognized you in those thoughts you wrote in those love notes. There were also a few other clues."

The waitress walked up and asked what we would like to drink. Jacob ordered two glasses of white wine. "But I was so careful to disguise my writing. I hid everything." Then I felt such intense emotions well up inside me that I started to cry. A tear ran down my cheek. He grabbed my hand and held it tightly between both of his hands.

"Oh, honey, why are you crying? Don't you know how much I love you?" I tried to wipe the tear from under my eye.

"I just wanted to add some excitement into my life, to feel more important than the person who did the laundry, taxi the kids, cook a meal. Then this idea popped into my head, and it sounded so alluring and fun. I put some thought into it and believed it would be adventurous, but when you didn't mention the love notes, I thought I opened a Pandora's box. Oh, Jacob, I'm sorry that I put you through this!"

"Sorry, don't be sorry. I loved your pursuit of me." He wanted to say more, but the waitress was approaching with our drinks. Jacob asked her for a few more minutes before she took our order, but he did tell her that she could begin with salads for us. He quickly gave her our dressing choices and off she went.

"I have to admit that the first few letters threw me. I wasn't sure who it was. Then I reread the letters over and over. I knew this person. She wasn't a stranger. She knew me and appreciated me. She shared the same life as me. She shared the same values, and I was happy that she shared the same home." A demure smile crossed my face. He leaned over and kissed me.

"Oh, baby. I am so happy. I thought our relationship was growing, but when you didn't mention receiving the puzzle pieces and the letters, I thought I really messed up."

"Speaking of puzzle pieces…" He released my hand, leaned over to the other chair, and pulled out a box. He handed it over to me. I slid it on the table and lifted the top. Inside was an eight-by-ten picture frame with the puzzle put together. It was just missing the final pieces. In the bottom right corner, written on the glass, it said, "Happy 15th!" He had been doing some planning himself. I looked at him in awe. Then he took the frame, turned it over, took off the back, and inserted the final pieces into place.

"There, now all the pieces are in place," he said triumphantly. He looked up at me, smiled, and added, "Now what would you like to eat? I'm sure our waitress will be back soon."

He handed me a menu. I opened it, but my mind was whirling. I stared at the menu but was really trying to process everything. He spoke, "I'm having the prime rib. Have you decided?"

"That sounds delicious," I said. The waitress approached us with our salads, and Jacob placed our dinner order.

As soon as the waitress left, he said, "I'll trade you that picture, which is really mine, for what is in box number two." He leaned over to the other chair and pulled out another box and handed it to me with his right hand while he took the picture box with his left hand. "This is for my office desk." He said as he put the picture in the box and haphazardly put the lid on it and set it on the other side of the table. Then he looked directly into my eyes and said, "Happy anniversary. Open it!"

This box had no wrapping paper but a simple satin bow. I pulled the ribbon, and it easily untied. I let out a little laugh as I opened it and saw a Baume and Mercier watch resting inside. It was delicate and feminine. "I love it. It's perfect," I spoke softly. I pulled it from the box, and he helped me put it on. Our waitress brought our meal. Once she walked away, I seductively whispered, "I have someone for you too. You'll have to wait until we get home." He raised his eyebrows up and down a few times. "Well, it's in addition to that." I smiled as I spoke. My heart was calm and happy. All the anxiety was gone. Jacob and I enjoyed our meal, and we talked about the letters and the puzzle. The conversation lasted until we drove home. The kids were asleep, and Jacob drove Katie home. I quickly slipped into a black teddy and brushed my teeth. I took the extra pillows off of the bed and lowered the coverlet. Then I took his gift from my dresser and placed the box on his pillow.

It didn't take Jacob long for him to return as I heard the door open and close. He walked into the bedroom as he was taking off his suit jacket. He closed the bedroom door quietly and locked it. He looked in my direction as I lay on my side. He glanced at his pillow. "What's this?" he questioned.

"It's the additional something," I said as he unbuttoned his shirt and removed it. Then he slithered out of his pants and slid his head toward me like a dive. He slipped his arm underneath me and in one motion pulled our bodies close together. "Wait, I want you to open your present," I stated.

"That's what I'm doing," he confirmed.

I laughed and said, "The box on your pillow." I reached for the box and handed it to him. He opened it and said, "We do think alike, baby. I love it! But I love you a whole lot more." He turned and started kissing me. Oh, how I love this man.

So even though there were so many emotions, I followed through with my plan. I don't think I will test our thirtieth anniversary when it comes. Time is just meant to be enjoyed—past, present, and future. Marriage is supposed to be faithful and final. I see all the pieces of our lives fit together as a puzzle (funny that is what I chose for my seductive plan), and we get to assemble them as a team. I can truly say I am content, happy, and loved. My puzzle is complete.

About the Author

Janet L. Adams lives with her husband, Paul, in Longview, Texas. They have two adult children, Amy and Brett, and are adding to their growing family. She was raised in Erie, Pennsylvania, alongside four sisters and one brother. Her educational career included teaching and school counseling.

She believes that life lessons can be collected through all experiences, good or bad. Faith, family, and friends drive her life.